PACKAGING SECRETS UNVEILED

PACKAGING SECRETS UNVEILED

SAKET SARAF

Worldwide Published by

Pendown Press

PENDOWN PRESS LLP
An ISO 9001 & ISO 14001 Certified Co.,
Regd. Office: 3767A, Kanhaiya Nagar,
Tri Nagar, Delhi-110035
Ph.: 8130886000, 9650072927, 8595249536
E-mail: info@pendownpress.com
Branch Office: 1A/2A, 20, Hari Sadan, Ansari Road,
Daryaganj, New Delhi-110002
Ph.: 011-45794768
Website: PendownPress.com

First Edition: 2024
Price: ₹399/-
ISBN: 978-93-5554-916-7

Layout and Cover Designed by Pendown Graphics Team
Printed and Bound in India by Thomson Press India Ltd.

Dedication

This book is dedicated to my father, Shri Prem Prakash Tauji & Shri Krishna Kr Bhaiji who have been the pillars of my life and have taught me everything I know. Your guidance, support and values are the foundations of my success.

Contents

CHAPTER - 1

"Origins: Tracing the Roots of My Journey" From 15000 to 200 Crores

Hello, dear readers, I am beyond excited and delighted that you have this book in your hands.

With this book, your journey in the F&B and QSR business domain will change forever.

Before I take you on that memorable journey to engage all your senses, a journey that will not only delight you but also make a world of difference to your packaging & tableware business, I assure you that with this book, you will be able to stand out amongst your competitors and carve a niche of success and profits for you.

However, before we delve into the mesmerizing world of F&B (more specifically QSR) and its profitable packaging secrets, allow me to introduce myself and share with you my journey which has had its share of ups & downs like all entrepreneurs.

The Essence of the Journey

My journey has led me to learn some great life and business lessons that helped me to go from a salary of a mere 15000 Rupees to running a business with a turnover of nearly 200 Crores.

This journey led me to understand the pain points of my clients as well as their secret desires. Understanding their challenges and desires has in turn led me to devise solutions for them through experience, research & experimentation.

In this book, I share these learnings & experiences with an open heart to enable you to:

Elevate Your Brand With Thoughtful Packaging Solutions!

- With the content shared in this book, you will be able to rise above the challenges & clichés prevalent in the market and embrace innovative, sustainable, and brand-aligned packaging solutions

- These solutions will enable you to significantly enhance the customer experience and distinguish your QSR or café even in the competitive market.

Okay, so getting back to my journey, let me take you to the starting point of this journey- where it all began.

The First Chapter

I have been fortunate that my Janma Bhoomi (place of birth) & Karma Bhoomi (place of work) are both places of immense historical and spiritual significance. No matter what the circumstances, the invisible, protective hand of the almighty has always guided me through life.

The first two and a half decades of my story are set in Sitamarhi, Bihar. Life was good, our paternal business of textiles was doing well. Filled with excitement I began assisting my dad & uncle in the business while studying, when I was barely a teen story.

I worked in the business for close to 10 years. Growing up in the world of textiles, I learned the ropes from my dad. Those early lessons were the foundations that I stand on today. Those lessons weren't just about making deals; they were about grit, determination, and the value of hard work.

And Then Came the Curve Ball

Then life threw me a curveball, our business and family faced challenges and we had to shift to Surat, Gujrat.

Life wasn't easy, money was so tight. Those days taught me some more lessons in frugality and optimization of resources that I carry with me even today.

Especially during my time in Surat, where I had to walk miles just to save a few bucks. I would walk 3 kilometers to save just 3 rupees. Even basic things were a luxury back then. I had to think multiple times before buying even a packet of glucose biscuits.

Though resources were tight, spirits were high. But through it all, I held onto my dreams tightly, knowing that one day, I'd make something of myself.

And make something I did! I didn't just build a business; I built a movement. [I saw the writing on the wall – plastic was choking our planet, and something had to change.] But more about that later, let's continue with my journey. Then came another turning point.

The Turning Point

I received an opportunity to work under Shri Khemka Bhaiji a very respected businessman & resident of Varanasi. It was a God-sent opportunity indeed. The family decided that under the circumstances, this was a safe option and I accepted.

I began working with Bhaiji in the paper industry in 2005 at Saarthak Vanijya (formerly known as Khemka Papers), This proved to be an invaluable platform to cultivate my skills and acumen in the fast-paced world of paper-based business.

I joined as an account executive; my role was mainly that of a data entry operator.

However, thanks to the lessons learned earlier and their effective implementation at my workplace, I moved up the hierarchy speedily. Within a few years, I made it up almost to the position of accounts head. However, I felt that an accountancy profile was a bit under-appreciated.

Unless You Ask, The Answer is Always No

I wanted to be in a more active role and I decided to take action on my desire. I mustered up the courage to ask Bhaiji to shift me to a sales profile and fortunately, he agreed. Over the years, I climbed the corporate ladder to ultimately serve as the Head of Sales & Marketing, a position that was both challenging and rewarding.

My time at Saarthak Vanijya was instrumental in shaping my core business values, including relationship-building, ethical conduct, and nurturing talent within teams. My hands-on approach in leading my division enabled me to modernize and optimize sales and marketing strategies, utilizing data-driven insights for more precise decision-making.

My first posting was at the Varanasi branch. A branch that was bringing in a business of 6 Crores. With the help of my learnings from various officials of leading paper mills, within 7-8 years this branch was doing a business of 100 Crores.

So, how did I turn things around, you might wonder?

Solve Don't Just Sell

Well, the paper market in those days was a seller's market, today we know and abide by the fact that "Customer is King"- unfortunately not in those days. In those days the customer used to come to the seller and they had a lot of pain points that were not being catered to.

With the help and support of JK Paper Mill & ITC Paper Mill officials, I understood & resolved the customers' pain points and I went out into the market, right into the interiors instead of waiting for the customers to come to us and this customer-centric approach reaped in a lot of success and happy customers.

Key to my growth was seizing every available opportunity and cultivating a mindset of ownership. This proactive approach was foundational in introducing contemporary business practices to the organization. It laid the groundwork for my later success in co-founding

Greenpack, particularly by fostering my expertise in channel distribution, sales planning, and key account management.

Business Flows in My Blood

Now for some years, I had been itching to get into business and every 3-4 years I would go to my Tauji (Elder Uncle) with a business proposal and he would shoot it down saying, work for some more time.

Coming from a traditional family where the elder generation's word was considered the law, I would follow what he said.

Finally, one day I took to him the proposal for Greenpack, by then I had a friend and the CEO of a paper mill ready to invest in my business. Also, an experienced CA from Khemka ji's office helped me draft a business plan and guided me to a government scheme offering a collateral-free 2 Cr loan.

To my surprise or rather pleasant shock, this time Tauji said yes but with a caveat that reaffirmed my learning that values and ethics are more important than profits!

Ethics Over Profits Any Day

He said that if I intended to go into business on my own, the first right of refusal lies with Bhaiji (Khemka Ji), the man who was responsible for my professional rebirth.

I was in a dilemma; how to approach my employer and ask him to become a business partner? It was unheard of!

I was hesitant but I knew this was the only ethical thing to do and I finally mustered the courage to ask him and again to my surprise and immense gratitude, he said YES!

That's when Greenpack was born, with a mission to shake up the food packaging industry with eco-friendly solutions.

Go Where the Ball Will Land: Go Green

So how did we decide to go in for paper packaging & tableware solutions?

Somebody had once told me that don't stay where the ball is, move to where the ball will land. This stayed with me.

At the time we were zeroing in on a business, concerns about plastic and its impact on the planet were rising. Customers were becoming aware of the negative impact of single-use plastic. And that is when I made it my mission to contribute toward reducing single-use plastic.

My approach wasn't just about making a profit; it was about making a difference.

I set up factories across India, not only to expand but to spread the message of sustainability far and wide.

And at the heart of it all was Varanasi, a symbol of my roots and vision for a greener future. My spiritual companion in the material world- My *Karma Bhoomi.*

My Mool Mantras

What has seen me through this journey from an employee of 15000 Rs to running a business of 200 Cr. are certain principles- my success mantras. And through these, I've built a company culture that's as innovative as it is ethical and successful.

- My big mantra of "avoid analysis paralysis" isn't just about making quick decisions; it's about trusting your gut and taking action. If you just keep planning and analysing and take no action, you will never get started.

- Don't wait for perfection, it doesn't exist. What you don't know, you can learn on the way, like I did. [My biggest challenge was the manufacturing side of the business because I did not come from an engineering background. I did not even understand the M of manufacturing or machinery, but I learned on the job, when I started Greenpack, I spent the initial year on the shop floor understanding all the technical processes. Interacting with and learning from my plant supervisor and even my machine vendors.]

- Team building, delegation & trust are essential to the success of a business, find and nurture the right people, delegate and trust them. It is impossible to do it all on your own. [In my case, I often joke that it is my innate laziness that has proven to be a boon for me, my excellence at team building and delegation stems from not wanting to do work, instead being good at getting work done].

My Living Legacy

Today I am propelling my mission of reducing the impact of single-use plastic on the planet forward with 3 plants- 1 in Varanasi, 1 in Ahmedabad and 1 in Kasna, Greater Noida. Toward this mission, we have scaled up 4 times in 4 years. This is all thanks to my team because this dream certainly wouldn't be a reality without them.

The Varanasi facilities are the bedrock of our operations with the largest production capacity among all our factories. The Ahmedabad plant specializes in LDPE Coated Reels & Sheets, effectively meeting the demand for diverse paper-based food containers, including cups and boxes.

The latest milestone came with the inauguration of our third plant in Greater Noida, in 2023. With a focus on innovation, this factory is engaged in manufacturing a new array of products like Ripple Paper Cups, Double Wall Paper Cups, Paper Bowls, and even Burger Boxes.

This plant is a testament to our commitment to innovate and diversify, always staying ahead of market trends and demands.

Today Bhaiji is proud to share my story of how his employee earning 15000 is today his business partner, and I am eternally grateful to him for his belief in me and for always having my back.

Also, it may sound cliché but challenges are indeed the stepping stones to success.

If life hadn't thrown me the curveball that made me move out of Sitamarhi, I probably wouldn't have reached the place that I am today.

I don't measure my success in crores or factories; it's measured in the smiles and well-being of future generations.

My story isn't just about success; it's about hope – hope for a planet where businesses care as much about people as they do about profit.

Now that you know me well, let me take you on that journey of the senses and packaging success that I promised at the beginning of the book.

Stay excited and stay with me to embark on a business-altering journey.......

CHAPTER - 2

Welcome To Flavor Town

In a lively place called Flavor Town, where you can find delicious food at every turn, these days there's a special story about the magic of a very unique type of packaging that's trending.

This isn't just any ordinary packaging; it's something that can make eating food an even bigger adventure and a memorable experience by making all your senses come alive.

This story shows how the right packaging can make you feel, see, hear, smell, and taste food in amazing new ways.

So, let's end the wait and let our story unfold:

Chef Sensoria, the hero of our tale, is famous for her delicious food. But she believes that eating should be about more than just taste. She wants to make eating a full experience that engages all your senses.

To do this, she teams up with Saket Saraf, a creative packaging expert, to make a special kind of packaging that does just that.

Saket suggests that in the bustling world of quick service restaurants (QSRs) and food delivery, the packaging of your meal does a lot more than just keep it safe and warm.

Imagine it as that secret ingredient that can make your food experience even more exciting! This is because the packaging can talk to your senses - especially when you feel it with your hands and consume it catch with your eyes.

Let's unwrap how smart packaging makes eating from your favorite QSR or delivery service even better, why it really matters, and some cool tips to make these experiences pop.

In the following chapters, you will discover the secrets of packaging used by Global QSR Chains to drive customer satisfaction & business success.

Always Remember - Food & Packaging are Like Chacha Chaudhary & Sabu. Always Complementing Each – Other.

CHAPTER - 3

Sensory Engagement - Unlocking the Power of Touch and Sight in Packaging

- **Activation of Touch Sensors:** Feeling the Food Before You Taste It

    - **What The Food Offers:** The texture of food, whether it be crunchy, smooth, or creamy, contributes significantly to the eating experience.

    - **What Packaging Adds:** The feel of the packaging could be used to add to the sensory experience by making it like the food inside.

If the snack is crunchy, the package could be customized to feel a bit rough to get you ready for that crunch.

Additionally, the ease of opening, the feel of the packaging in your hand, and even resealability features can enhance convenience and tactile interaction. The feel of the right temperature maintained through the right packaging ignites desire and enhances hunger.

1. **Activation of Sound Sensors:** Setting the Scene

    - **What The Food Offers:** The sound of food, such as the crunch of chips or the sizzle of bacon, can be amazingly appetizing and deeply satisfying.

    - **What The Packaging Adds:** Opening the package also has its own special sound. This sound ignites your auditory senses and gets you ready for the fresh taste.

2. **Activation of Smell Sensors:** Getting Your Nose Ready

    - **What The Food Offers:** The aroma of food is a key component of its flavor. Freshness and quality often have distinct smells that are integral to the food's appeal.

 – **What The Packaging Adds:** Packaging that controls airflow can help preserve the food's aroma until it's opened. When you open the package, it releases a tantalising hint of the food's smell.

It's just enough to make you really look forward to the first bite. Imagine opening a cookie package and getting a whiff of that baked cookie smell.

3. **Activation of Visual Sensors:** A Feast for the Eyes

 – **What The Food Offers:** The visual presentation of food, including its color, texture, and arrangement, significantly impacts our desire to eat it. We often "eat with our eyes" first.

 – **What The Packaging Adds:** High-quality, visually appealing packaging design can enhance the food's perceived value and quality. Clear windows in packaging allow the product to be seen, adding to the visual appeal and trust in the product's freshness. The use of vibrant colors and imagery can also stimulate appetite and desire.

4. Activation of Taste Sensors: The Big Moment

- **What The Food Offers:** The inherent flavors of the food, whether it be sweet, salty, sour, bitter, or umami, create the primary taste experience.

- **What The Packaging Adds:** With all your other senses already enjoying the experience, the taste of the food feels even better. The packaging plays a crucial role in keeping the food fresh, so when you finally eat it, it's exactly as delicious as you hoped.

The Importance of Sensory Activation

Sensory activation has many benefits that elevate eating food into a holistic and pleasurable experience as shared below. Creating this experience for your customers will lead to brand loyalty and business success.

- **Emotional Connection:** Engaging sensory experiences can create a stronger emotional connection between the consumer and the product, enhancing brand loyalty and recall.

- **Perceived Value:** High-quality, sensory-activating packaging can elevate the perceived value of a product, allowing for premium pricing and positioning.

- **Competitive Differentiation:** In a crowded market, products that offer a unique sensory experience can stand out, attracting more attention and driving sales.

CHAPTER - 5

Getting Packaging Right -Global Tips for Indian Fast-Food Places

Welcome back to the bustling world of Flavor Town, where every meal is an adventure and the packaging is the unsung hero of our food journey.

Chef Sensoria and her friend, the wizard in packaging, are on a mission. They want to show Indian quick-service restaurants, or QSRs, how changing the way they package their food can make a big difference.

This chapter, "Getting Packaging Right," is their guide to doing just that.

To put into perspective the importance and value of packaging, consider the misplaced use of ripple cups, designed with the intent to safeguard hands from the scorch of hot beverages, now being repurposed to serve cold coffee.

This not only defeats the purpose of its design but also detracts from the consumer's experience, as the thermal properties of the cup are mismatched with the contents it holds.

Then, there's the saga of the long tubs, an elegant solution for certain delicacies, turned into a cumbersome challenge for both the eateries serving and the patrons consuming.

These tubs, while visually appealing, make the simple act of serving and eating a logistical puzzle, detracting from the joy of the meal.

Also, lets not forget how the overzealous application of the tape, intended as a seal of safety, morphs into a barrier, instilling a fear of spillage as consumers struggle to unveil the treasure within.

This excessive fortification, rather than reassuring, becomes a reason for frustration, dampening the initial excitement of the meal.

Breathability, or rather the lack thereof is another criminal F&B mistake. Think about the crushing disappointment when a crispy snack turns soft and mushy.

This happens because the packaging doesn't let air in. Without air, what was once crunchy and enjoyable becomes soggy and unappealing.

Then, there's the problem with how food is placed in these packages. ***Sometimes, food that should lay flat is squeezed into a package standing up,*** which messes it up. It's like trying to fit something into the wrong space – it just doesn't work. ***The food gets squished and doesn't look or feel how we expected.***

Another big mistake is not considering the shape and whole look of the food. ***Packaging should fit the food perfectly, not the other way around.*** But often, food is forced to fit into unsuitable packaging, changing its shape and ruining the eating experience.

Let's dive deep into this and learn how to avoid the mistakes which are being made by 9/10 of Indian QSRs in selecting their packaging. Remember these packaging mistakes are draining your profits and killing your brand silently.

CHAPTER - 6

Section 1 – Beverages

Served in Cups

Hot Beverages (Cutting Chai - Chai Tea – Coffee - Other Hot Beverages)

Temperature Retention

Use longer Shapes

Use Insulated Cups like – Ripple or Double wall Cups

Structural Integrity (Easy to Hold)

Use Higher Gsm of Paper so neither it gets pressed easily nor hands get burnt

Use Cup 125% the capacity of the portion served

Use cups not more than 7degrees of angle

Premium Presentation

Use Food Safe Quality Paper with good printability.

Use Double Wall Paper Cups

Use Paper / Bagasse Lids

Use a Kraft Inner Cup

Easy to drink

Use a Sipper

Use a Heavier Rim of paper cup

Leak Prevention

Use Good Quality Barriers like PE or Aquas

Use Cups made from Double Blade Raw Materials

Use Cups with Both Side Coated Bottoms

Unadulterated Taste

Use Food Safe Paper Use Food Safe Barrier & Use Food Safe and odourless Ink.

Transforming the Tea Drinking Experience with Greenpack's Innovative Paper Cup Revamp

A Case Study

Following changes:

- **Material Upgrade:** Greenpack spearheaded a comprehensive upgrade by introducing clay-coated paper with enhanced thickness for improved heat insulation. This upgrade ensured that the cups were more comfortable and safer to hold, even with hot beverages.

- **Size Adjustment:** The cup size was increased to allow space at the top, minimizing spillage risk and providing a cooler area for handling.

- **Clear Communication:** Additionally, clear markings indicating "Hot Area" and "Hold Area" were incorporated for effective communication, further enhancing user experience and safety.

- **The Amazing Result:** The holistic approach implemented by Greenpack resulted in an immediate and tangible improvement in the customer experience:

  - **Enhanced Safety:** The redesigned cups significantly reduced the risk of spills and provided a safer and anxiety-free tea-drinking experience for customers.

- **Improved Comfort:** With better heat insulation and ergonomic design, customers found the cups more comfortable to hold, contributing to heightened satisfaction during their tea-drinking ritual.

- **Renewed Confidence:** Witnessing the positive impact of the cup revamp, the client gained renewed confidence in Greenpack's expertise and extended their collaboration.

• **Expansion and Continued Partnership:** The success of the paper cup revamp paved the way for a broader collaboration between Greenpack and the café chain. Entrusted with revamping the entire range of paper cups, Greenpack continued to innovate, ensuring that every touchpoint of the customer experience was enhanced.

• **Conclusion:** Greenpack's commitment to enhancing everyday experiences through thoughtful innovation was exemplified in the successful transformation of the café chain's paper cup range. By addressing the challenges with creative solutions, Greenpack not only improved safety and comfort but also contributed to a more enjoyable tea-drinking experience.

As a dedicated partner, Greenpack remains committed to bringing innovative solutions to the table, ensuring that every sip is a delight for customers in the bustling world of Chaï - café culture.

Cold Beverages

[Requires Refrigeration (Lassi – Milkshake – Buttermilk)]

- **Temperature Retention**

  – Use Broader Shapes

  – Use Both sideCoated Cups or Double Wall Cups

- **Structural Integrity (Easy to Hold)**

  – Use Standard Gsm of Paper so it doesn't get pressed

  – Use a Cup with 110% capacity of the portion served

  – Use cups not more than 7 degrees of angle

- **Premium Presentation**

  Use Quality Paper with good printability.

  Use Double Wall Paper Cups

  Use Paper Lids

  Use a Kraft Inner Cup

- **Easy to drink**

  – Use Wider Paper Straws

  – Use Dome Shaped Lids

- ## Leak Prevention

    – Use Cups made from Double Blade Cut Raw Materials

    – Use Cups with Both Side Coated Bottoms

- ## Unadulterated Taste

    – Use Food Safe Paper

    – Use Food Safe Barriers

    – Use Food Safe and odourless Ink

- ## Cold Beverages

    – [Does Not Require Refrigeration But requires Ice] (Iced Tea - Cold Coffee - Soft Drinks)

- **Temperature Retention**

  – Use Standard Shapes

  – Use Both side Coated Cups or Double Wall Cups

- **Structural Integrity (Easy to Hold)**

  – Use Paper made for freezer applications

  – Use Standard GSM of Paper so it doesn't get pressed

  – Use Cup 110% of the portion served

  – Use Cups not more than 7 degrees of angle

- **Looks Premium**

  – Use Paper with good printability.

  – Use Single Wall Paper Cups

  – Use Paper Lids

- **Easy to drink**

  – Use Wider Paper Straws

  – Use Dome Shaped Lids to accommodate top-ups like cream etc

- **Leak Prevention**

  - Use Good Quality Both Side Barriers like PE or Aquas

  - Use Cups made from Double blade cut Raw Materials

  - Use Cups with Both Side Coated Bottoms

- **Unadulterated Taste**

  - Use Food Safe Paper

  - Use Food Safe Barriers

  - Use Food Safe and Odourless Ink

CHAPTER - 7

Section 2 – Foods

A. Served in Bowls

- **With Thick Gravy -** Paneer (Cottage Cheese)/Chicken Gravy, Chole (Chickpeas Curry), Rajma (Kidney Beans Curry) Bhaji (Spicy Mashed Vegetable Gravy), Missal [Served with Pav /Bread], Pasta, Noodles, Dahi Bhalla, Raj Kachori, Papdi Chat, Aloo Tikki Etc

- **With Thin Gravy –** Sambar (Lentil-based Vegetable Stew), Kadhi Pakora (Yogurt-based Curry with Fried Vegetable Fritters), Dal (Lentils), Khow -suey, Fish Curry Rasogulla, Ras Malai, Lal Mohan – Kala Jamun Etc

- **Temperature Retention**

    - **Shape Optimization:** Use Smaller radius Shape of Bowl,

    - **Insulating Materials:** Consider using Bowls made from Paper with low thermal conductivity into the paper pulp, such as bamboo fiber, which is not only sustainable but also offers excellent thermal properties.

    - **Insulating Air Pockets:** Creating designs that incorporate air pockets between layers of paper can significantly improve insulation. This method uses the air as an insulator, similar to double-glazed windows.

- **Structural Integrity (Easy to Hold)**

  - **High-Quality Paper Stock:** Use high-strength paper fibers that can withstand moisture and heat without weakening. Virgin fiber paper, while more expensive, offers superior strength and heat resistance compared to recycled fibers.

  - **Optimized Bowl Design:** The shape of the bowl can significantly impact its structural integrity. A rounded base with smooth curves distributes stress more evenly than angular designs, reducing the risk of collapse. Additionally, incorporating ribbing or embossing on the bowl's walls can enhance stiffness and resistance to deformation.

- **Premium Presentation**

  - **High-Quality Paper:** Opt for superior-quality paper with a smoother finish. The texture and finish of the paper significantly impact the premium feel. A brighter, whiter base paper can also make colors and prints stand out more vividly.

  - **Sustainable Materials:** Incorporating eco - friendly materials like bamboo, bagasse, or recycled paper can add to the premium appeal, as modern consumers increasingly value sustainability.

– **Custom Design Features:** Adding embossed patterns, and Gold / Silver foiling can enhance both the visual appeal and functionality.

– **Proportional Design:** Well-proportioned bowls that balance depth and diameter convey a sense of deliberate design. Compact and sleek designs often appear more premium than bulky ones.

– **High-Quality Printing:** Utilize high-definition printing techniques to add intricate designs, brand logos, or custom artwork.

– **Minimalist Design:** A trend towards minimalism in packaging design can also convey premium quality. Simple, clean designs with ample white space and subtle color palettes can suggest sophistication and elegance.

- **Easy to Eat**

  - **Ergonomic Design:** Opt for shapes that are not only visually appealing but also functional. A slightly curved bottom inside the bowl can make it easier for spoons or forks to pick up food, ensuring minimal waste and ease of eating.

  - **Rim Design:** Consider designing the rim of the bowl to be slightly outward or rolled to provide an easy grip and prevent spills. This design can also help in holding the bowl when the food is hot.

  - **Appropriate Sizing:** Offer a variety of sizes tailored to different types of meals or food items, ensuring that the depth and width facilitate easy access to the food without causing discomfort or inconvenience.

- **Leak Prevention**

  - **Seamless Design:** Opt for a bowl design with minimal seams. Seams are potential weak points where leaks can start, so a design where seams are strategically placed away from direct contact with liquids can help prevent leaks.

– **Reinforced Structure:** Incorporate an additional layer of Coating or a thicker coating in the bottom of the bowl. This reinforcement acts as a robust barrier, especially in the area most susceptible to puncture or degradation from hot contents.

– **Double-Blade Cut Raw Materials:** Incorporating cups made from double-blade cut raw materials into your product lineup can significantly enhance the quality and performance of your paper cups. This manufacturing technique involves the precise cutting of paper materials using a double-blade system, ensuring uniformity and precision in the dimensions of the cups.

B. Served in Boxes

For foods that are juicy, saucy, or have a risk of spilling, leak-proof packaging is essential to maintain quality and ensure customer satisfaction without messy accidents.

- **Temperature Retention**

  Using Thicker Paper or corrugated paper can help in greater retention of Heat.

- **Structural Integrity (Easy to Hold)**

  Using high-strength Virgin fiber Kraft paper can help

in enhance stiffness and resistance to deformation.

- **Premium Presentation**

  - **Sustainable Materials:** Incorporating eco-friendly materials like bamboo, bagasse, or recycled paper can add to the premium appeal, as modern consumers increasingly value sustainability.

  - **Proportional Design:** Well-proportioned bowls that balance depth and diameter convey a sense of deliberate design. Compact and sleek designs often appear more premium than bulky ones.

  - **Minimalist Design:** A trend towards minimalism in packaging design can also convey premium quality. Simple, clean designs with ample white space and subtle color palettes can suggest sophistication and elegance.

- **Easy to Eat**

  - **Wider Opening:** Opt for shapes that are not only visually appealing but also functional.

  - **Appropriate Sizing:** Offer a variety of sizes tailored to different types of meals or food items, ensuring that the depth and width facilitate easy access to the food without causing discomfort or inconvenience.

• **Leak Prevention**

  – **Seamless Design:** Opt for a bowl design with minimal seams. Seams are potential weak points where leaks can start, so a design where seams are strategically placed away from direct contact with liquids can help prevent leaks.

Overcoming Packaging Challenges in the QSR Industry with Greenpack Solutions

A Case Study

- **The Objective:** To address packaging issues faced by a Quick Service Restaurant (QSR) chain, specifically concerning oil and grease seepage affecting food presentation and customer satisfaction.

- **The Client:** A prominent QSR chain grappling with packaging challenges impacting the presentation and quality of their products.

- **Challenge:**

  - **The Challenge:** The QSR chain's purchase manager, Mr. Sharma, identified a pressing issue with their packaging. Despite offering delicious burgers and sandwiches, the packaging was failing them, resulting in an unappetizing messy presentation and customer dissatisfaction. Complaints were on the rise, necessitating a swift and effective solution.

  - **The Focused Audit:** The audit by the Greenpack team revealed that the MG Poster Paper being used for packaging was unable to contain the butter, oil, and grease. This was all seeping through the packaging to create a messy and unappetizing food delivery/presentation.

- **The Innovative Solution:** Greenpack responded to the challenge with a comprehensive approach tailored to the client's needs:

  - **Switch to OGR Paper:** Greenpack introduced Oil and Grease Resistance (OGR) paper, which effectively prevented oil and grease from seeping through, ensuring clean and hygienic packaging for the food and customers' hands.

  - **Incorporating Parchment and Aqua-Based Barrier Coated Papers:** For products requiring specialized care, such as baked goods, Greenpack recommended parchment paper known for its non-stick properties. Additionally, an aqua-based barrier-coated paper was introduced for other items, offering excellent moisture resistance while being environmentally friendly.

- **The Amazing Result:** The implementation of Greenpack's solutions led to immediate and noticeable improvements:

  - **Enhanced Customer Satisfaction:** Customers appreciated the neat and grease-free packaging accompanying their favorite meals, resulting in increased satisfaction levels.

- **Boost in Repeat Visits and Positive Reviews:** Mr. Sharma reported a significant uptick in customer satisfaction metrics, leading to higher rates of repeat visits and positive reviews for the QSR chain.

- **Successful Transformation:** The swift resolution of packaging challenges underscored Greenpack's commitment to offering innovative, practical, and sustainable solutions tailored to the unique needs of its clients.

• **The Conclusion:** The successful collaboration between Greenpack and the QSR chain exemplifies the impact of addressing packaging challenges with innovative solutions. By implementing OGR paper, parchment paper, and aqua-based barrier-coated papers, Greenpack not only improved the presentation and quality of the client's products but also enhanced the overall customer experience.

This case remains a proud moment for Greenpack, highlighting its dedication to enhancing client satisfaction and delivering tangible results in the competitive QSR industry.

Now you know, what to avoid and what to do to ensure you get your packaging right. You must have observed that there are lots of Paper, Coating and Printing details you need to know to get your packaging Right

Ready to become a packaging pro?

- In the 1st Section, we will discuss about the types of Papers available and you will get to know a lot about those in detail.

- In the 2nd Section, we will discuss about the types of Barrier Coatings available & you will get to know a lot about those in detail.

- In the 3rd Section, we will discuss about the types of Printing and Inks and you will get to know a lot about those in detail.

Excited? Let's dive in!

You have to Understand the importance of selecting the right paper type for your food packaging needs. Here's a comprehensive overview of the various types of paper used in paper-based packaging along with their pros and cons:

1. Cup Stock Board Paper:

Cupstock paper board is a specialized material designed specifically for the production of disposable cups, including those used for hot and cold beverages. This type of paper board is engineered to provide the necessary structural integrity, moisture resistance, and thermal properties required for holding liquids without leaking or becoming too hot to handle.

Here's an in-depth look at the Cupstock paper board, detailing its layers, materials, and characteristics, as well as its advantages and disadvantages. **Layers and Materials**

Cupstock paper board typically consists of several key layers, each serving a specific purpose:

- **Top Layer (Food Contact Layer):** Made from virgin bleached pulp to ensure purity and safety for direct food contact. This layer provides structural integrity and stability to the paper, ensuring that the cup or bowl maintains its shape and rigidity.

- **Middle Layer(s):** Comprised of a mix of virgin and recycled fibers to provide bulk and stiffness to the board. This layer is crucial for giving the cup its structural strength and insulation properties, especially important for hot beverages.

– **The Bottom Layer (Printing Surface):** This layer is smooth and designed for printing, allowing for brand logos and designs to be applied directly onto the cup.

• **Characteristics**

– **Strength:** Cup Stock Board Paper is engineered to offer exceptional strength and durability, making it well-suited for withstanding the rigors of handling and transport associated with food packaging.

– **Molding Capabilities:** Due to its composition and manufacturing process, Cup Stock Board Paper exhibits excellent molding capabilities, allowing it to be formed into various shapes and sizes with precision and ease. This makes it the ideal choice for producing paper cups and bowls with intricate designs and details.

– **Moisture Resistance:** Due to High Edge Wick, it is better than other uncoated grades of paper, in low absorption of moisture and grease, ensuring that the integrity of the packaging is maintained even when in contact with liquids or oily substances.

- **Printability:** Cup Stock Board Paper provides a smooth and consistent surface for printing high-quality graphics, branding elements, and product information, allowing for attractive and informative packaging designs.

- **Best Suited Industries**

  - **Quick Service Restaurants (QSRs) and Cafés:** Perfect for disposable cups used for coffee, tea, soft drinks, and other beverages.

  - **Fast Food and Takeaway Outlets:** Anywhere that offers drinks on the go can benefit from the convenience of Cupstock-based cups.

  - **Event and Catering Services:** Ideal for one-time use in settings where easy cleanup and disposability are valued.

- **Pros**

  - **Customization and Branding:** Offers excellent opportunities for branding, as the cups can be printed with custom designs and logos.

  - **Convenience:** Lightweight and disposable, making them perfect for fast-paced food service environments.

  - **A Variety of Coating Options:** Allows for selection based on environmental impact, cost, and performance requirements.

- **Cons**

  - **Cost Variability:** The price can fluctuate based on the raw material and coating type chosen, impacting overall product cost.

  - **Temperature Limitations:** Cups designed for hot beverages may not perform as well with cold drinks, and vice versa, unless specifically designed for both.

Cupstock paper board represents an essential material for expanding into or enhancing a range of disposable cup products. By leveraging the characteristics of Cupstock, you can meet the needs of QSRs, cafés, and other food service outlets looking for high-quality, customizable, and potentially eco-friendly disposable cups. Balancing the pros and cons of different coatings and materials within the Cupstock category will enable you to offer products that align with consumer preferences for convenience, quality, and sustainability.

2. Clay Coated Cup Stock Board Paper:

Clay Coated Cup Stock Board Paper is an enhanced grade of CupStock paper specifically designed for food packaging applications, particularly for items like paper cups and bowls. This grade of paper features a layer of clay coating applied to the Cup Stock Board, offering several benefits:

- **Enhanced Printability:**

The clay coating on Cup Stock Board Paper significantly improves its printability compared to uncoated alternatives. The smooth surface provided by the clay layer allows for crisp, vibrant printing of branding elements, graphics, and product information. This ensures that packaging designs are visually appealing and attention-grabbing, enhancing the overall presentation of the product.

- **Improved Smoothness:**

The clay coating also contributes to the overall smoothness of the paper surface. This smooth texture not only enhances the appearance of the packaging but also improves the tactile experience for consumers when holding the packaging. The smooth feel adds a sense of quality and professionalism to the product, making it more enjoyable to handle and interact with.

Overall, Clay Coated Cup Stock Board Paper is a premium-grade packaging material that combines enhanced printability, smoothness and consumer-friendly packaging solutions for a wide range of food products. Its ability to elevate branding and provide an enjoyable consumer experience makes it an excellent choice for businesses looking to stand out in the competitive market.

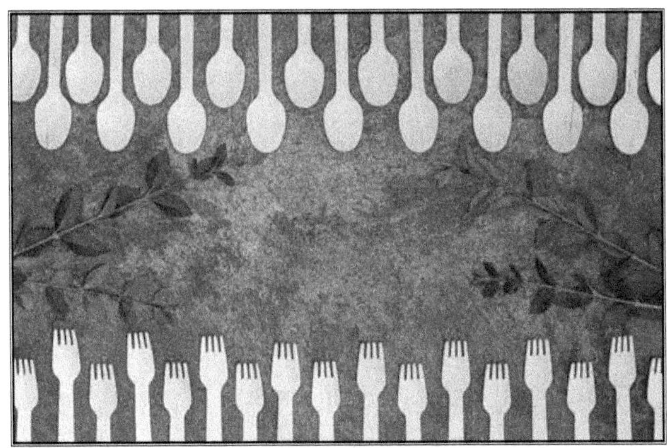

3. Folding Box Board (FBB):

Folding Box Board (FBB) is a type of paperboard that's particularly favored for its light weight, high stiffness, and excellent printing surface, making it an ideal choice for premium packaging solutions.

FBB is widely used across various industries, including the food, pharmaceutical, cosmetic, and consumer goods sectors, due to its versatility and quality.

Here's a comprehensive overview of FBB, covering its structure, composition, and characteristics, as well as its advantages and disadvantages, tailored to provide insightful information for you.

- **Layers and Materials**

Folding Box Board is typically composed of multiple layers that are:

  - **Top Layer (Coated Surface):** The outermost layer is made from high-quality bleached chemical pulp, which provides a smooth, white surface that's ideal for high-quality printing and graphic reproduction. This layer is often coated with minerals such as kaolin clay to enhance its smoothness, brightness, and printability.

  - **Middle Layer(s):** The middle layer or layers are made from mechanical pulp, which includes both thermo-mechanical and chemi-thermo-mechanical pulps. This layer is crucial for providing bulk and stiffness to the board, which is essential for its structural integrity and durability.

– **The Back Layer:** The back layer, which might also be coated, is usually made from the same bleached chemical pulp as the top layer but with less emphasis on smoothness and whiteness. This layer contributes to the overall strength and stability of the board.

- **Characteristics**

  – **Excellent Printability:** Thanks to its smooth, coated surface, FBB offers superior printability, allowing for vibrant, detailed graphics.

  – **Good Stiffness and Strength:** The combination of chemical and mechanical pulps provides FBB with excellent stiffness and strength, ensuring durability.

  – **Lightweight:** FBB is lighter than other types of paperboard, making it cost-effective for shipping and handling.

  – **Recyclability:** FBB is recyclable, aligning with increasing demand for sustainable packaging solutions.

  – Best Suited Industries

  – **Cosmetic and Perfumery Packaging:** The high-quality print surface makes it ideal for the visually appealing packaging required in these sectors.

– **Pharmaceutical Packaging:** Suitable for packaging where strength, durability, and cleanliness are paramount.

– **Food Packaging:** Especially for dry foods, chocolates, and frozen foods where the packaging's visual appeal is crucial.

– **Luxury Goods Packaging:** The premium look and feel of FBB make it perfect for luxury items like jewelry, watches, and high-end electronics.

• **Pros**

– **Superior Aesthetics:** Enables high-quality printing and finishing options, enhancing brand presentation.

– **Environmental Sustainability:** Made from renewable resources and is recyclable, offering an eco-friendly packaging option.

– **Versatility:** Can be easily cut, creased, and formed into a variety of packaging shapes and sizes.

– **Cost-Effectiveness:** The lightweight nature reduces shipping costs, and its strength allows for using less material without compromising on quality.

- **Cons**

  - **Moisture Sensitivity:** Less resistant to moisture compared to other boards like Cup Stock Board, requiring additional treatments for certain uses.

  - **Limited Rigidity Compared to Thicker Boards:** While stiff, FBB may not be as rigid as thicker corrugated boards, potentially limiting its use for heavy or bulky items.

For You, incorporating FBB into your product lineup could significantly enhance the range of premium packaging solutions you offer, especially for segments in the QSR, café chain sectors, and beyond. Its outstanding printability and aesthetic appeal can elevate product presentation, aligning with consumer expectations for quality and sustainability. Understanding FBB's unique properties will enable you to effectively meet the diverse needs of your clientele, leveraging both its advantages and navigating its limitations to provide tailored, high-quality packaging solutions.

4. **Duplex Board:**

   Duplex board, often utilized in the packaging industry for its versatility and durability, is a type of paperboard or cardboard. It is called a "duplex" because it is made up of two layers, or plies, which are usually made from wood pulp with a combination of recycled paper fibers. The structure and composition of the duplex board give it unique properties and functionalities, making it suitable for a wide range of applications, particularly in the food packaging and fast-moving consumer goods (FMCG) sectors. Here's a detailed overview of the duplex board, breaking down its layers. materials, characteristics, and its advantages and disadvantages for various industries, including how it might suit your operations.

- **Layers and Materials**

A duplex board is composed of two main layers:

- **Top Layer (Coated Side):** This layer is usually made from wood pulp, which provides a smooth white surface that is ideal for high-quality printing. The top layer is often coated with materials like kaolin clay or calcium carbonate to improve its brightness, smoothness, and printability. This coating also makes the board more resistant to moisture and grease.

- **Bottom Layer (Uncoated Side):** The bottom layer is typically made from recycled paper materials, contributing to the board's strength and rigidity. This layer is uncoated and has a greyish or white colour. It gives the board its structural integrity and makes it more sustainable due to the incorporation of recycled materials.

• **Characteristics**

- **Strength and Durability:** Duplex board is known for its strength and durability, making it resistant to crushing and bending.

- **Printing Surface:** The coated surface of the duplex board provides an excellent base for printing, allowing for vibrant and detailed graphics.

- **Eco-Friendliness:** The use of recycled materials in the bottom layer makes duplex board a more sustainable packaging option.

• **Best Suited Industries**

- **Food Packaging:** Ideal for packaging dry and greasy food items like cereals, snacks, and fast food due to its moisture and grease resistance.

- **Pharmaceuticals:** Used for packaging medicines and healthcare products that require a clean, safe, and durable packaging solution.

- **Cosmetics and Personal Care:** Offers an attractive and sturdy packaging option for beauty and personal care products.

- **FMCG Products:** Suitable for packaging a wide range of consumer goods, including household items and electronics, that demand high-quality print for branding.

• **Pros**

- **Cost-Effective:** Duplex board is a cost-effective packaging material, especially compared to other high-quality, print-friendly options.

- **Sustainability:** Incorporating recycled materials makes it a more environmentally friendly option.

- **Customizability:** Can be cut, folded, and shaped into various packaging solutions, offering versatility.

• **Cons**

- **Limited Moisture Resistance:** While it has some moisture resistance, it's not suitable for very wet or frozen products without additional treatments or barriers.

- **Print Quality Variances:** The quality of the recycled material in the bottom layer can sometimes affect the overall print quality and board uniformity.

- **Food Safety:** Due to recycled materials used, there are concerns about Food Safety, if it comes directly in contact.

The duplex board could serve as an excellent material for producing packaging solutions that require high-quality printing and durability, such as for your range of food packaging products. Its versatility and sustainability align with the growing demand for eco-friendly packaging solutions, particularly in the QSR and café chain sectors. Leveraging the strengths of the duplex board while navigating its limitations can help in tailoring packaging solutions that meet the specific needs of your clients in these industries.

5. **Cupstock Kraft (Bamboo) Paper:**

   Cup stock Kraft (Bamboo) Paper represents a specialized subset of kraft paper that is increasingly gaining attention for its sustainable and environmentally friendly attributes, especially in the disposable cup industry. Made primarily from bamboo pulp, this type of cup stock offers an eco-friendly alternative to traditional wood pulp-based papers without compromising on quality or functionality. Here's a comprehensive overview of Cup stock Kraft (Bamboo) Paper, its composition, characteristics, and suitability for various industries, with a focus on how it could benefit operations like Greenpack India Private Limited.

- **Composition:**

  - **Material:** Cupstock Kraft (Bamboo) Paper is primarily composed of a blend of bamboo fibers and Kraft pulp derived from softwood trees. This combination enhances the paper's strength and resilience while reducing its environmental impact.

  - **Function:** Cupstock Kraft (Bamboo) Paper is engineered to withstand the rigors of food packaging, providing a sturdy and reliable barrier against moisture, grease, and other external factors. It is specifically designed for use in the production of paper cups, bowls, and other disposable food containers.

- **Characteristics:**

  - **Strength and Durability:** Cupstock Kraft (Bamboo) Paper offers excellent strength and durability, making it suitable for the manufacturing of paper cups that can withstand the heat and weight of hot and cold beverages. It maintains its structural integrity even when exposed to liquids and oils, ensuring that the contents remain securely contained.

  - **Sustainability:** Bamboo fibers are known for their rapid growth and renewability, making Cupstock Kraft (Bamboo) Paper a sustainable alternative to traditional paper materials. By incorporating bamboo fibers into the paper composition, manufacturers can reduce their reliance on finite natural resources and minimize environmental impact.

  - **Printability:** Cupstock Kraft (Bamboo) Paper provides a smooth and printable surface for branding, logos, and other graphics. It accommodates various printing techniques, allowing for customized designs and messaging to enhance brand visibility and appeal.

- **Industries Best Suited For:**

  - **QSR and Café Chains:** Ideal for disposable cups, both hot and cold, emphasizing environmental sustainability without sacrificing quality.

  - **Event and Catering Services:** For events prioritizing eco-conscious choices, bamboo cup stock offers a disposable yet environmentally responsible option.

  - **Eco-Friendly Packaging:** Beyond cups, this material can be used for packaging products where sustainability is a key selling point.

- **Pros**

  - **Environmental Impact:** One of the most significant advantages is its reduced environmental impact compared to traditional paper sources.

  - **Renewable Resource:** Bamboo is a highly renewable resource, with certain species capable of growing up to 91 cm (36 in) within a 24-hour period.

  - **Compost ability:** When coated with biodegradable materials, the end product is fully compostable, aligning with zero-waste goals.

- **Versatility and Aesthetic Appeal:** The natural look and feel of bamboo paper can enhance the product's aesthetic appeal, aligning with brands that promote natural and organic values.

- **Cons**

  - **Cost Considerations:** Depending on sourcing and processing, bamboo cup stock can be more expensive than traditional wood pulp-based alternatives.

  - **Barrier Performance:** While inherently somewhat moisture-resistant, additional coatings are necessary for liquid containment, which may affect compostability depending on the materials used.

  - **Supply Chain Complexity:** The sourcing and production of bamboo pulp might involve more complex supply chains, especially in regions where bamboo is not a native crop.

Integrating Cup stock Kraft (Bamboo) Paper into your offerings could significantly bolster your portfolio's sustainability credentials. This material aligns well with the growing consumer and corporate demand for eco-friendly disposables, especially in the QSR, café, and catering industries. By adopting bamboo-based cup stock, you can provide your clients with a product that not only meets their practical needs but also supports their environmental objectives. Balancing the pros and cons, especially around cost and supply chain considerations, will be key to successfully implementing bamboo cup stock as a viable alternative in your product lineup.

- **Oil and Grease Resistant (OGR) Paper:**

Oil and Grease Resistant (OGR) paper is a specialized packaging material designed to prevent oil, grease, and moisture from penetrating the paper, making it ideal for wrapping and packaging oily or greasy foods. This feature is crucial for maintaining the integrity of both the packaging and the food product, ensuring that the customer experience is not compromised by leaks or sogginess.

Here's a detailed exploration of the OGR paper, including its composition, characteristics, suitability for various industries, and its pros and cons, tailored for applications like those at Greenpack India Private Limited.

- **Composition and Layers**

OGR paper can be made from a variety of base paper materials, including but not limited to kraft paper, and is characterized by its treatment to resist oils and greases:

  - **The Base Layer:** Typically consists of a high-quality paper base, such as kraft paper, which provides the primary structure and strength of the packaging.

  - **Coating or Treatment:** The key feature of OGR paper is its treatment or coating with materials that provide resistance to oil and grease. This can be achieved through various means, including fluorocarbon treatments, silicone coatings, or the application of specialized barrier coatings that are designed to repel oil and grease.

- **Characteristics**

  - **Oil and Grease Resistance:** The primary characteristic, as the name suggests, is its ability to resist penetration by oils and greases, protecting the product and preventing messes.

- **Suitable for Direct Food Contact:** OGR papers are generally safe for direct contact with food, an essential characteristic for food packaging.

- **Customizable:** Can be produced in various weights, and thicknesses, and with different levels of oil and grease resistance, depending on the specific needs of the application.

- **Printability:** Offers good printability, allowing for branding and product information to be easily applied.

- **Best Suited Industries**

  - **Fast Food and QSRs:** Ideal for wrapping items like burgers, shawarmas, rolls, samosas, and other greasy foods.

  - **Bakeries and Snack Shops:** Suitable for packaging baked goods that may contain or be coated with oils or butters.

  - **Food Markets and Delis:** Can be used to wrap meats, cheeses, and other deli products that may release oils or moisture.

- **Pros**

  - **Enhances Product Integrity:** Keeps the food safe and ensures that the packaging remains clean and presentable.

- **Improves Customer Experience:** Prevents grease stains and leaks, making it easier for customers to handle and consume on-the-go foods.

- **Versatile:** Can be used for a wide range of food products, enhancing its utility for businesses that offer a variety of oily or greasy foods.

- **Sustainability Options:** Some OGR papers are available with eco-friendly coatings, catering to the growing demand for sustainable packaging solutions.

- **Cons**

  - **Cost:** OGR paper can be more expensive than standard paper options due to the specialized treatments or coatings required.

  - **Environmental Considerations:** Traditional oil and grease-resistant treatments may involve chemicals that are not environmentally friendly, although more sustainable options are increasingly available.

  - **Recyclability:** The presence of certain types of oil and grease-resistant coatings can complicate recycling processes, although this varies depending on the specific materials used.

Incorporating OGR paper into your product lineup could significantly enhance the quality and appeal of your packaging solutions for oily and greasy food items. This material aligns with the needs of QSRs, cafes, and other food service outlets seeking high-quality, functional packaging that maintains food integrity and enhances the customer experience. Balancing the selection of OGR paper—considering factors like cost, performance, and sustainability—will be key to meeting the diverse needs of your clientele while supporting your commitment to quality and environmental responsibility.

CHAPTER - 9

Coating It Right

As a Paper packaging Expert, I also understand the pivotal role that sustainable, biodegradable coatings play in the paper-based tableware industry, especially for environmentally conscious businesses like QSR and café chains.

The movement towards eco-friendly materials is not just a trend but a necessity, and selecting the right coating for your paper-based tableware products is crucial.

Here's a structured guide to some of the most promising biodegradable coating options, designed to help purchase managers and business owners make informed decisions.

1. **Polylactic Acid (PLA) Coating**

   – **Summary:** PLA is a compostable polymer derived from fermented plant starch, offering a greener alternative to traditional PE coatings.

- **Suitability:** Ideal for cold to moderately warm food packaging, such as cold drink cups, salad bowls, and non-heated food containers.

• **Pros:**

- **Compostable:** Breaks down in industrial composting facilities within 3-6 months.

- **Renewable:** Made from corn or sugarcane, promoting the use of sustainable resources.

- **Non-Toxic:** Safe for direct food contact.

• **Cons:**

- **Heat Sensitivity:** Can deform at temperatures above 110°F (45°C), limiting its use for hot foods.

- **Composting Requirements:** Needs industrial composting facilities to break down efficiently.

- **Fun Fact:** PLA is often used in 3D printing, showcasing its versatility beyond packaging.

2. Water-Based Coatings

- **Summary:** These coatings are environmentally friendly, emitting no VOCs and are composed of water as the solvent base.
- **Suitability:** Good for packaging products intended for foods and beverages that are not exposed to high heat, such as bakery items and cold drinks.

- **Pros:**
  - **Compostable:** Breaks down easily in compost environments.
  - **Safe Production:** Lowers environmental impact with no VOC emissions.
  - **Neutral Impact:** Odorless and tasteless, preserving food quality.

- **Cons:**
  - **Heat Resistance:** Not suitable for very hot foods but can handle temperatures suitable for tea or coffee.
  - **Market Presence:** Less common in the market, which may affect availability.

Fun Fact: Water-based coatings are also used in the art world for their safety and low environmental impact.

3. Beeswax Coating

- **Summary:** A natural coating derived from beeswax, offering excellent barrier properties against moisture and grease.

- **Suitability:** Best for wrapping solid food items like cheeses, sandwiches, and for containers holding cold or room-temperature foods.

- **Pros:**

  - **Natural and Compostable:** Fully biodegradable and home compostable.

  - **Barrier Properties:** Effective against grease and moisture.

- **Cons:**

  - **Cost:** More expensive than synthetic alternatives.

  - **Heat Sensitivity:** Not suitable for packaging hot food items due to melting risk.

  - **Fun Fact:** Beeswax has been used for centuries in various applications, from cosmetics to waterproofing.

4. Starch-Based Coatings

- **Summary:** Derived from natural starches, these coatings are an affordable, biodegradable option for food packaging.

- **Suitability:** Suitable for dry food packaging, such as for chips, nuts, and cereals.

- **Pros:**

  - **Biodegradable:** Breaks down naturally in the environment.

  - **Cost-Effective:** Less expensive compared to other eco-friendly coatings.

  - **Food Safe:** Generally recognized as safe for direct food contact.

- **Cons:**

  - **Moisture Resistance:** Less effective compared to other coatings, limiting its use with very moist or greasy foods.

  - **Commercial Scalability:** Still developing in terms of wide-scale commercial application.

  - **Fun Fact:** Starch is not just for coatings; it's also a key ingredient in bioplastics, demonstrating the versatility of natural materials.

For QSR and café chain owners, understanding the balance between environmental responsibility, functionality, and cost is key to selecting the right biodegradable coating for your paper-based tableware.

Each option presents a unique set of benefits and challenges, tailored to different types of food packaging.

Whether prioritizing compost-ability, barrier properties, or cost-effectiveness, there's a sustainable coating solution that aligns with your brand's values and operational needs.

**The terms "biodegradable" and "compostable" are often used interchangeably, but they are indeed different*

Decoding Biodegradability:

- **Definition:** A biodegradable material can be broken down by natural processes into basic components like water, carbon dioxide, and biomass.

- **Timeframe:** The breakdown period can be highly variable and is not strictly defined. It could take from months to years.

- **Environmental Impact:** Biodegradable products may still produce harmful residues or methane gas during decomposition, especially in landfills.

Understanding Compostability:

- **Definition:** Compostable materials not only break down but also add valuable nutrients to the soil during the composting process.

- **Timeframe:** Typically, compostable items decompose within a composting cycle of around 90 to 180 days.

- **Environmental Impact:** Composting ensures that the material breaks down in a way that is beneficial to the environment, usually in industrial composting facilities under controlled conditions like temperature and humidity.

Understanding these differences is critical, especially for businesses like yours. It helps make more informed choices for your products and communicate those benefits effectively to your customers.

CHAPTER - 10

Inking It Right

In the competitive landscape of QSR and café chains, the visual appeal of your packaging can significantly influence customer perception and brand experience.

Understanding the nuances of printing types and ink options for paper-based tableware is crucial for any business looking to stand out.

Here's an expanded guide that includes offset printing alongside flexographic and digital printing methods, complete with ink types used in each process, to aid purchase managers and business owners in making well-informed decisions.

Printing Techniques for Paper-Based Tablewares

1. **Flexographic Printing**

   – **Summary:** Utilizes flexible printing plates for high-speed, efficient printing on various materials.

   – **Suitability:** Best for large-volume orders of cups, napkins, and takeaway boxes, requiring quick turnaround and consistency.

- **Pros:**

   – **Cost-Effectiveness:** Ideal for large runs due to lower per-unit costs.

   – **Speed and Efficiency:** High printing speeds make it suitable for tight deadlines.

   – **Versatility with Inks:** Compatible with a wide range of inks, including eco-friendly options.

- **Cons:**

   – **Quality Limitation:** Typically offers lower resolution than digital or offset printing.

   – **Initial Setup Costs:** Higher upfront costs for creating printing plates.

2. **Digital Printing**

   – **Summary:** Directly prints digital images onto tableware, allowing for high-detail and customizable prints without the need for plates.

- **Suitability:** Perfect for short runs or custom designs, such as limited edition tableware or items with specific event branding.

- **Pros:**

  - **High-Quality Prints:** Offers vibrant, detailed images with excellent resolution.

  - **Design Flexibility:** Easy to modify designs without incurring significant additional costs.

  - **Quick Setup:** Minimal setup time required, reducing lead times.

- **Cons:**

  - **Higher Cost for Large Volumes:** Per-unit cost remains constant, making it less economical for large orders.

  - **Ink Limitations:** Not all digital printing inks are suitable for direct food contact.

3. **Offset Printing**

  - **Summary:** Offset printing transfers ink from plates to a rubber blanket, and then to the printing surface, allowing for high-quality, efficient production.

  - **Suitability:** Ideal for high-volume, high-quality print jobs requiring precise color and detail, such as branded tableware and custom packaging designs.

- **Pros:**

  - **Exceptional Quality:** Produces sharp, clean images with consistent color.

  - **Cost-Efficiency for High Volumes:** More economical for large quantities compared to digital printing.

  - **Versatility:** Can print on a wide range of substrates with various ink types.

- **Cons:**

  - **Setup Time and Cost:** Requires more setup time and higher initial costs for plate production.

  - **Less Flexible for Short Runs:** Not as cost-effective for small quantities due to setup requirements.

Ink Types for Paper-Based Tablewares

1. **Water-Based Inks**

   - **Used in:** Flexographic and Digital Printing

   - **Summary:** Eco-friendly inks that use water as a solvent, offering a safer alternative for food packaging.

- **Pros:**

  - **Eco-Friendly:** Low VOC emissions and better for recycling.

- **Food-Safe:** Generally considered safer for direct food contact.

- **Cost-Effective:** Lower cost compared to solvent-based or UV inks.

- **Cons:**

  - **Drying Time:** Longer drying times can slow production speed.

  - **Durability:** May not offer the same level of durability as UV-curable inks.

2. **UV-Curable Inks**

   - **Used in:** Digital and Offset Printing

   - **Summary:** Inks that dry instantly when exposed to UV light, providing durability and resistance.

- **Pros:**

  - **Instant Drying:** Enhances production efficiency with quick curing times.

  - **High Durability:** Resistant to smudging, water, and fading.

  - **Versatile Applications:** Suitable for a variety of packaging types.

- **Cons:**

  - **Cost:** Generally more expensive than water-based inks.

- **Safety and Environmental Concerns:** Requires careful handling due to potential safety risks.

3. **Soy-Based Inks**

    - **Used in:** Offset Printing

    - **Summary:** Made from soybeans, these inks are an eco-friendly alternative to petroleum-based inks, offering vibrant colors and easier recycling.

- **Pros:**

    - **Environmental Benefits:** Lower VOC emissions and promotes easier de-inking during recycling.

    - **Print Quality:** Produces rich, vibrant colors with good rub resistance.

    - **Renewable:** Made from a renewable resource, reducing dependency on petroleum.

- **Cons:**

    - **Cost:** Can be more expensive than traditional inks, though prices are becoming more competitive.

    - **Drying Time:** May have longer drying times compared to traditional and UV-curable inks.

For QSR and café chain owners, selecting the appropriate printing method and ink type is a strategic decision that impacts not just the aesthetics of your tableware but also its environmental footprint and cost-effectiveness.

Whether you prioritize the unparalleled quality of offset printing, the efficiency and versatility of flexographic printing, or the customization and detail of digital printing, pairing it with the right ink can enhance your brand's presentation while adhering to sustainability practices.

CHAPTER - 11

Navigating the Lesser Evil: Single-Use Paper Over Plastic for a Greener Tomorrow

Let's face it: we all know single-use plastics are bad news for the environment.

They clog our oceans, endanger marine life, and take hundreds of years to decompose. But hold on! Before you pat yourself on the back for switching to single-use paper, let's get the facts straight.

- **Single-Use Paper:** While better than plastic, it's not a guilt-free pass. It still consumes energy and natural resources to produce.

- **The Lifecycle:** If we look at the life cycle analysis, single-use paper items are not as eco-friendly as you might think. They often end up in landfills. We all need to put effort into recycling the same.

- **The Lesser Evil:** If we must choose between two evils, single-use paper is still the far better option. It decomposes much quicker than plastic, usually within weeks to months.

Why Do Restaurants Still Swipe Right on Paper Packaging?

Ah, the age-old debate: Paper or Plastic? It's like choosing between a sturdy, reliable partner and a fun, unpredictable relationship.

Let's break down the details, shall we?

- **Team Plastic's Selling Points:**

  - **Superhero Durability:** Plastic is the Superman of food packaging. It's strong, almost indestructible, and can handle hot, cold, and everything in between.

  - **Barrier Beast:** Got moisture? Oxygen? Plastic says, "Not on my watch." It doesn't let anything pass through.

- **But Wait, Team Paper Isn't All Roses:**

  - **Leakage Drama:** Imagine having a paper cup of coffee, and halfway through, it pulls a Titanic and starts sinking. Yeah, paper can be 'leaky' like that gossiping colleague.

- **Performance Anxiety:** Put something too hot or too moist into paper, and you might see it crumble faster than a cookie in milk.

- **So Why Do Restaurants Still Choose Paper?**

  - **Eco-Warrior:** Paper is that friend who insists on carrying a reusable water bottle and shops second-hand. It's the eco-friendly choice we all aspire to be.

  - **Sophisticated Suitor:** Plastic may be functional, but paper has that premium, "I read books and drink artisan coffee" vibe.

  - **Political Correctness:** With bans on plastic gaining momentum, paper is like that friend who always knows the right thing to say.

  - **Laughs in Customization:** Paper lets you doodle, print, and brand like you're Picasso with a printing press. It's conducive to customization.

Yes, we know, even our paper packaging has had its "Oops, did I do that?" moments. But just like that cousin who's terrible at keeping secrets but amazing at planning parties, we love paper for its charms, not its imperfections!

QSRs still choose it because it's the less harmful option for the planet!

CHAPTER - 12

How to get more customers from an online delivery programme and make your customer repeat their orders by 45% through its packaging.

- **Beware of These Seven Industry Clichés:**

  - **Fast food means fast forgettable packaging:** This mindset overlooks packaging's potential as a branding powerhouse. Opt for custom, eco-friendly packaging that leaves a lasting impression and aligns with consumer values.

  - **Cheaper is better for the bottom line:** While cost-efficiency is important, cheap packaging can compromise food quality and customer experience. Invest in quality, sustainable options that reflect your brand's commitment to excellence.

– **Eco-friendly packaging doesn't impact customer choice:** Today's consumers are more environmentally conscious than ever. Utilizing biodegradable and recyclable materials can significantly influence customer loyalty and attract a broader audience.

– **One-size-fits-all packaging works for any menu:** Customization is key in packaging as much as it is in your menu. Tailor your packaging to your specific offerings to ensure food integrity and enhance the dining experience, even on the go.

– **Packaging innovation isn't a priority for QSRs:** In an era where experience is everything, innovative packaging solutions that offer convenience, sustainability, and style can set your café or QSR apart from the competition.

– **More is always better when it comes to packaging:** This cliché can lead to overpackaging, contributing to waste and environmental harm. A minimalist approach that focuses on efficiency and sustainability can be more effective, reducing waste and often enhancing the customer experience by demonstrating a commitment to environmental responsibility.

– **Packaging is just a container, not a branding opportunity:** Underestimating the branding potential of packaging is a missed opportunity. Innovative and branded packaging not only serves as a protective container for food but also as a powerful marketing tool that communicates your brand's identity, values, and message directly to your customers.

• **Elevate Your Brand with Thoughtful Packaging Solutions**

Challenging these clichés and embracing innovative, sustainable, and brand-aligned packaging solutions can significantly enhance the customer experience and distinguish your QSR or café in a competitive market. Consider the following strategies to elevate your brand:

– **Invest in Sustainable Materials:** Show your commitment to the environment by choosing biodegradable, recyclable, or compostable packaging.

– **Embrace Customization:** Use packaging to reinforce your brand identity through custom designs, shapes, and materials that reflect your unique offerings and values.

– **Prioritize Innovation:** Stay ahead of industry trends by adopting innovative packaging technologies and designs that improve functionality, sustainability, and customer engagement.

– **Optimize for Experience:** Ensure that your packaging not only looks good but also enhances the dining experience with convenience, functionality, and reliability.

Navigating the Path to Sustainable Satisfaction with Greenpack

A Client Experience Story

A Quest for Sustainability

In the dynamic world of cafe ownership, the pursuit of sustainability is both a passion and a challenge. For one of our valued clients, this journey began with a desire to transition from plastic to eco-friendly paper lids without compromising on functionality.

- **Expectations vs. Reality: Challenges Unveiled**

Excitement, however, turned to apprehension when the client discovered that the paper lids didn't match the sealing capabilities of their plastic counterparts. Concerns arose regarding functionality and customer satisfaction.

- **Listening and Responding: A Client-Centric Approach**

At Greenpack, customer feedback is paramount. Swift action was taken to replace the batch of paper lids, ensuring uninterrupted service. However, it became evident that a more comprehensive solution was required.

- **Collaborative Solutions: Partnership in Progress**

Engaging in open dialogue, our teams collaborated

to understand the client's unique needs. Through this partnership, an alternative product from our range emerged as a promising solution, aligning sustainability with functionality.

- **Triumph in Adaptation: A Perfect Fit**

The alternative solution exceeded expectations, seamlessly blending functionality with environmental benefits. The client's delight and loyalty were evident, reinforcing the value of collaboration and adaptation.

- **Beyond Cost, Towards Value: Investing in Satisfaction**

While for us at Greenpack, there was a cost associated with this journey, the true gains lay in customer satisfaction and relationship reinforcement. Every challenge presented an opportunity to reaffirm our commitment to our client's success, and we didn't hesitate to put client satisfaction first.

- **A Journey of Growth: Learning and Commitment**

This experience served as a reminder that challenges are catalysts for growth. At Greenpack, we remain dedicated to understanding our clients' needs and delivering tailored solutions, no matter the distance we must travel.

We're more than just a supplier; we're partners in your sustainable journey. With a relentless commitment to understanding and adapting, we stand ready to navigate the path to satisfaction alongside our clients, one eco-friendly solution at a time.

CHAPTER - 13

Choosing Your Path

Now that we have come to the end of this book, please know that this is just the end of the book, not the end of our journey together.

I have shared the secrets of global packing solutions that all the prominent and successful QSR chains in the world use. And I have shared all this in detail right down to the inks being used.

With this book as your ready reference guide, you are well-equipped to make the necessary changes to your packaging solutions and step onto the path of success.

However, for those of you, who want your success to be smoother and faster, I have a surprise gift for you.

Register with us for an audit of your current packaging solutions. We will do this audit for you completely FREE, identify the gaps & suggest the best success solutions for your QSR business.

Send us a mail: Saket@greenpackindia.com

www.ingramcontent.com/pod-product-compliance
Lightning Source LLC
Chambersburg PA
CBHW050548160726
48003CB00002B/812

9 789355 549167